# THE COMPLETE GUIDE TO

# RENTING AN RV

By Jeff Wildrick

Campground reviews    3/2020

www.Campgroundreviews.com

www.Camp pendium

*With love for my favorite traveling companions:*

*my wife (and editor), Kathy, and our kids, Natalia, Jhony, and*

*Angela. Thanks for the fun we've had RVing, and the patience*

*you've had with me during writing and publishing.*

*Now let's get ready for our next trip!*

ISBN-13: 978-1519784896
ISBN-10: 1519784899

# Table of Contents

# INTRODUCTION

So you're thinking about renting an RV. Congratulations! The allure of RVing is almost intoxicating. The freedom of the open road. The dream of seeing America from ground level, and enjoying all of the majesty and quirkiness you encounter along the way. The excitement of campfires, roadside picnics, and getting close to nature. The opportunity to spend quality time with your family away from work, school, and the siren call of chores you need to do around the house. RVing holds the promise of one of your most relaxing or exciting vacations of all time.

But then you remember those movies you've seen, such as RV starring Robin Williams, and a certain level of doubt or fear starts to creep in. Will we all be able to get along together in such a small space? (Or will I be safe on the road alone?) How do I choose the right RV (recreational vehicle) to rent? How do I find it? Where will we go? How do I drive that thing? What about the poop!

For a vacation that's all about life's simple pleasures, the challenge of renting and planning an RV vacation can be daunting. I should know. I've been there! The first time we rented an RV, I was overwhelmed by the number of choices I had to make before we even left home. What did I need to know about the many different kinds of motorhomes available for rent? How would we find places to stay at night that brought smiles instead of grimaces? And I'd never driven anything larger than a minivan! So I began to research anything and everything I could think of about RVing. Frankly, my family accused me of being obsessed. "Dad, you're not reading about RVs again!" But I was determined to give my family (and myself) the very best RV vacation possible.

It must have worked, because after that first RV trip in Arizona, even my most cynical teenage daughter said, "That was the best vacation EVER. When can we do it again?"

What I quickly learned when planning an RV vacation was that there is a lot of information out there. That was an exciting discovery. On the other hand, there's really no one place you can go to learn all that you need to know about planning the best RV vacation for your family, your vacation, and your needs. My goal here is to bring it all together to give you the benefit of my research, mistakes, and discoveries.

Many different kinds of RVs are available to fit a wide variety of needs. For the purposes of this book, when I use the term "RV" I'll be referring to a self-contained motorhome—one vehicle that contains both living space and an engine to drive it around. (The other kinds of RVs are "travel trailers" and "fifth wheels," which are towed behind a pickup truck or large car. Most of this book will still be relevant, except for some of the discussion about selecting a motorhome.)

This book is a step-by-step guide to planning and enjoying the best possible RV rental vacation. Whether you've rented before, or you're a true first-timer, you'll find the information you need to have the kind of vacation that leaves you and your family asking for more. All charts and tables in the book are available free to download from www.completervrentalguide.com.

Happy travels!

# CHAPTER 1—CHOOSING THE RV THAT'S RIGHT FOR YOU

In considering an RV (recreational vehicle) vacation, the first and perhaps most important decision is choosing an RV. Where should you even begin?

Well, what's the one thing you'll spend more time doing in your RV than driving? Chances are that the answer is sleeping, which means that choosing a sleeping configuration that fits your family and your needs is the most important decision you will make when renting.

For instance, in our family a "must have" is four separate beds. With a teenage boy and two teenage girls, the boy needs a bed of his own, and the two girls, who have separate bedrooms, aren't going to be happy sharing a small double bed for a week or more. So, even if an RV is advertised as sleeping five, if two of those five are sharing a fold-out bed in the RV's living area, our family is not going to have a happy vacation. On the other hand, my wife and I can be comfortable for a week or more in a full-, queen-, or king-size bed in an RV's "master bedroom." If you're sharing a bed and the two of you can't get a good night's sleep in anything less than a king, that's pretty important! I happen to sleep with a CPAP machine, and I quickly discovered that many RVs don't have shelves beside the bed (or only on one side). I have to have a shelf of some sort. I always carry an extension cord, too, in case there's no outlet near my side of the bed.

Fortunately, a wide variety of sleeping configurations are available. In the majority of rental RVs, you'll find that in addition to the bed in the master bedroom, you'll also be able to convert the dinette into a bed and the sofa into a bed. But don't assume that they will suffice for anyone. Check their dimensions! Our kids are relatively short, so it's not a big issue with us, but can you imagine how uncomfortable your six-foot-tall son is going to be if you need him to squeeze into a five-and-a-half-foot bed? Also realize that if you'll be using the couch or dinette area for beds, you'll need to set them up each night and break them down each morning to have your dinette and sofa available for the day.

One of the most distinctive features of some motorhomes (Class Cs in particular, to be discussed in the next section) is the bed that is found over the cab area. In smaller units this may be the only bed, but in larger units it provides a second full-size sleeping area accessible by ladder from the living area. When renting a Class C, this is where we like to place our son, who is harder to wake up than a mummy. He can sleep in while we convert the dinette and couch back into living space for breakfast and lounging.

A great feature to look for if you'd like to keep the living area the living area, and the sleeping area the sleeping area, is bunk beds. Even some mid-sized motorhomes are now building in a set of bunks, sometimes with each one even having its own mini TV. Really. At the moment these are few and far between, but they are a great alternative for families traveling with children.

The next step is to familiarize yourself with the three classes of RVs available for rent.

---

## Class A

A Class A motorhome is easily recognizable because it looks like a bus. Ranging in size from 25 feet to over 40 feet, Class As offer a number of appealing features. Starting at the front, Class A RVs have huge windshields that give you virtually a panoramic view of the beautiful countryside. The cockpit areas are usually large with big, comfortable chairs for driver and passenger. A relatively new feature in some Class A vehicles is an extra bed that drops down from the ceiling over the cockpit area once you are parked and set up for the night.

Because they are big, Class A coaches usually feel quite roomy. Most will have between one and four "slides" to provide even more room in the kitchen and living area when parked.

A slide is a portion of the RV that uses a small electric motor to literally slide out from the side of the coach, making that portion of the RV several feet wider. When you are driving, the slides must be in, and the living area or bedroom will be fairly narrow, with only a little room to walk up and down the length of the coach. When extended, the slides can give you more space in the living area, kitchen, or even the bedroom and bathroom at the back of the RV. When you're ready to break camp, just clear the floor, push the button, and watch your nice big home on wheels return to the size of a truck or bus.

Class A RVs come with either gasoline or diesel engines. While diesels may get better fuel mileage, the difference is probably not significant for the amount of miles you'll be driving a rental. Coaches with a gasoline engine are called "gassers," and the motor is in the front. "Diesel pushers" have their engines in the back, which leads to a quieter ride up front. They also give a smoother ride because of their air suspensions.

The primary sales market for Class A coaches is retired couples who want to take extended trips and want to have the room and some of the luxuries of home—things like residential refrigerators, a second half-bathroom, and extra counter space in the kitchen. This is why, despite their size, most Class As sleep fewer adults than even a smaller Class C, and far fewer Class As are available on the rental market at significantly higher cost.

The advantages of a Class A are centered around the word "comfort." The comfortable ride, upgraded amenities, power, and tremendous view from the cab contribute to a comfortable, sometimes even luxurious camping experience.

The disadvantages are mostly related to size. You do not need a special license to drive a big Class A rig in most states, but you certainly need to learn some special driving skills (see Chapter 8). Gas mileage is usually low. Still, nothing compares to the feeling of rolling down the road at the wheel of one of these beauties, and having many luxuries in a home-on-wheels once you stop.

## Class B

Class B RVs are built on a van chassis, so compact living is the word. It's simply amazing how much the designers can fit into such a small space! The biggest advantage of the Class B is drivability. If you can drive a van, you can drive one of these. And you can take them anywhere that a van can go. Class B rentals are surprisingly hard to find. This is bare-bones as far as motorhomes go, but they sure can be fun, and you'll really feel more like you are camping.

## Class C

Class C motorhomes are the bread-and-butter of the RV rental industry. These "big boxes" of the RV world come in all sizes and with just about every configuration you can imagine. Ranging in size from 20 to over 31 feet, the most distinctive feature is the cab-over extension that usually .s a bed.

Driving a Class C is like driving a medium-sized truck. In fact, driving a truck is the best comparison to driving one of these versatile vehicles. While the "house" is open to the cab, it usually has its own separate entrance. And the cab has a door on each side for passenger and driver. Almost all Class C RVs have Ford cabs and engines.

Most Class C motorhomes, like Class As, place the main bedroom in the far back, with a small kitchen in the middle and the living area up front, but smaller units will skip the bedroom and provide only a cab-over bed. Many Class Cs have a slide that increases the size of the living area when you are parked. The larger the unit is, the more amenities you are likely to find. There are so many alternative floor plans that you'll almost certainly be able to find one that fits your needs. There isn't as much outside storage as in a Class A, but when on a weeklong vacation, we've still never used it all.

The largest Class C is roughly the size of a small Class A, which means that they are much easier to maneuver through traffic and into campsites—although there is still a learning curve if you're stepping up from driving a car. Gas mileage is slightly better, too, but probably not as much as you'd expect.

---

## Bigger is Not Necessarily Better

No matter what class of motorhome you decide to rent, keep in mind that size matters. But bigger is not necessarily better.

As a first-time renter, it's unlikely that you'll be towing a car behind your motorhome to use for local transportation. But without a car, most RVers limit their local driving. It's just a lot of work to undo the hookups, stow the awning, bring in the slides, and maneuver out of a tight campsite with the prospect of driving a large vehicle out to visit an attraction or restaurant – only to come back to the campsite, maneuver in, hook up, extend the slides, and roll out the awning again when you return (possibly after dark).

This may be contrary to what you expect, but my advice is to rent the smallest motorhome that will meet all of your needs and most of your wants. It will be easier to drive, park, and maneuver. It will also get better gas mileage and will be a little easier to set up and break down.

And now the moment you've been waiting for. It's time to go online and start looking at rental RVs!

# CHAPTER 2—MAKING THE DEAL

There are a number of places you can go to rent a great RV, and each has its own benefits and liabilities.

---

## Chains & Brokers

The reason that most people rent their RV from a chain is simple: convenience. You can do almost all of your searching online, and you'll be dealing with people who do one thing and one thing only: rent RVs. A hidden advantage is that the bigger the chain, the more likely they'll have a unit available that meets your needs, and they'll be able to service your vehicle more easily if you have a breakdown. Finally, it is often easier to rent for one-way trips. These are the major RV chains:

### Cruise America (www.cruiseamerica.com):

The largest and most well known is "Cruise America." Their motorhomes are easily recognizable by the iconic scenes of nature and camping that literally wrap around their vehicles, as well as their name and website, of course. Why not advertise for free when on the road? Cruise America rents Class C RVs that have been custom built for them and come in four sizes: Compact, Standard, Intermediate, and Large. Their website is well laid out and gives good explanations of the benefits and floor plans of each model. Whenever I've spoken with their rental agents, they have been patient and well informed, and seemed truly committed to matching the right RV to their customers' needs.

Because Cruise America has custom designed their RVs for the rental industry, they've eliminated some features that are fairly standard in the buyer's market. For instance, on Cruise America RVs you will not find an awning or retractable steps up into the coach. The reason they've omitted these from their design is that they are the parts of an RV most often damaged by renters. Instead, they encourage you to bring a canopy of your own to set up at your campsite, and the first step into the motorhome from the ground is slightly higher than in comparable models.

Because Cruise America has over 120 locations, it is far easier to do one-way rentals than with many other companies, and sometimes you can even get a discount if they are trying to move vehicles in their fleet from one part of the country to another.

**El Monte RV (www.elmonterv.com):**

With 32 locations across the United States, El Monte comes in a distant second to Cruise America. At the time of this writing they offer four Class A models and nine Class C models to choose from, made by several different manufacturers. This means that you'll find a wide variety of floor plans and amenities to meet your needs, all of which are fully explained on their website.

**Road Bear RV (www.roadbearrv.com):**

With only seven locations (most on the West Coast), this small chain offers one Class A and three Class C models to choose from. They are known for their excellent customer service and the fact that they replace their entire fleet every year.

**Bates International (www.batesintl.com):**

In addition to their own fleet of RVs, this company acts as a broker for private individuals who wish to rent out their motorhomes. Their website lists hundreds of different late-model motorhomes to choose from in locations all across the country. The website is a bit difficult to navigate, but ultimately all the information you need is there, and the options are many.

**Camper Travel USA (www.campertravelusa.com):**

This company is a broker that specializes in helping domestic and international travelers find and rent an RV in the United States. Because it works with many different dealers, it is sometimes able to secure vehicles that are not listed as available on the dealer's website, and it can offer a low price guarantee. The website is easy to navigate, but you need to be aware that when you accept an online rental quote, you are not yet guaranteed a reservation. In other words, the online availability list is not posted in "real time." Camper Travel will contact the dealer during local business hours to confirm availability and then contact you to confirm the rental—and work hard to assure your satisfaction.

## Local Dealers

If you are planning a round-trip vacation, you will often find that the best prices are available from local RV dealers at your starting/ending point. Dealers will often make a portion of their stock available for rent, knowing that a lot of customers like to rent before they buy. But you don't need to be in the market to buy in order to rent from a dealer. They'll be happy to take your money either way!

Because dealers are primarily in the business of selling and servicing RVs, they may have only one or two people to handle their rental customers, and even they may only do so part time, so you may need to wait a little longer than with a chain to get a question answered. Their websites may not be as complete. But the price and personal service you receive may be well worth the wait. We actually had one occasion when a local dealer gave us a ride back to the airport, and because both he and we had time, he also gave us a tour of the city along the way.

The best way to find local dealers who rent RVs is to do an Internet search with the name of the city or region you'll be visiting and "RV rentals" or "motorhome rentals."

## Private Individuals

Motorhomes are expensive, and yet the majority of people who buy them end up using them only a few weeks at a time and a few weekends each year. The rest of the time the motorhome sits in the driveway or in storage while the monthly payments just keep on coming. So, it's no surprise that many individuals decide to let their RV start paying for itself by making it available for rent.

There are two ways to rent a private RV. The first is through a broker such as Bates International (www.batesintl.com), Private Motorhome Rentals (www.privatemotorhomerental.com), or Share My RV (California only—www.sharemyrv.com). The amount of assistance that the broker provides for you or the private owner varies.

You can also rent directly from the owner. Check the listings for "RV Rentals" on Craigslist in the area where you want to rent (www.craigslist.com). The advantages of renting from private owners include price, flexibility, and amenities. Since this is their personal RV, they will have it set up just the way they (and hopefully you) like it. Because the owner usually has only one motorhome, it will be available only when they are not using it, and when it's not already rented to someone else. Private owners may be more inclined to allow early pick-ups and late-drop offs or give rides to the airport. But the cleanliness and quality of the vehicle may vary based on the personality and meticulousness of the owner. And if the motorhome breaks down after you've driven a few hundred miles, you'll need to know how to get service and how it will be paid for.

## Compare Features

After making a decision about your sleeping needs, make a list of "must haves" vs. "wants" for the RV. As you browse the Internet looking at various RVs for rent, you'll probably find yourself being drawn back to one or two. Perhaps it's that great floor plan. Maybe it's the amenities. Maybe it just looks terrific and you think it would be fun to drive. Great! Narrow the list down to three or four possibilities if you can, then contact the owner, agent, or dealer to check on availability and get a price quote.

## Feature Comparison Chart

|  | Unit 1 | Unit 2 | Unit 3 | Unit 4 |
|---|---|---|---|---|
| Rental Company or Individual | | | | |
| RV Class (A, B, C) | | | | |
| Length | | | | |
| Sleeping Capacity | | | | |
| Total number of regular beds (King, Queen, Full, Twin) | | | | |
| Total number of short beds (and size) | | | | |
| Slides | | | | |
| Square Feet of Living Area | | | | |
| Interior Storage | | | | |
| Exterior Storage | | | | |
| TV/Entertainment | | | | |
| Microwave Oven | | | | |
| Convection Oven | | | | |
| Standard Oven | | | | |
| Number of Stove Burners | | | | |
| Refrigerator Size | | | | |
| Shower Size | | | | |
| Air Conditioning | | | | |

| Heating | | | | |
|---|---|---|---|---|
| Awning | | | | |
| Pet Friendly | | | | |
| Suitable for Boondocking | | | | |
| Pick up time | | | | |
| Return time | | | | |
| Other | | | | |

(A printable version of this chart can be downloaded free at www.completervrentalguide.com)

## The Rental Agreement

Whenever you receive a quote for a particular RV, you should receive a copy of the rental agreement along with the price, a list of what's included in that price, and a list of options along with how much each option costs. In all cases, it's your responsibility, and yours alone, to read and understand the terms of the rental agreement, and there is no industry standard. If you don't understand something, ask questions. Some terms are inherently subject to interpretation such as "clean." Who decides whether the vehicle is clean when you return it, and how will that be decided? What constitutes "normal wear and tear"? What constitutes a "rental day"? Is it a 24-hour period, or an overnight? The number of items that may not be covered in the base price for your rental is almost endless. Items for which you may be charged extra include:

- Miles driven over a certain number per day

- Bringing the unit back with waste in the black water or gray-water tanks

- Propane

- Generator usage

- Pets

- Sheets & towels

- Dishes and silverware, pots, pans, cooking utensils

- Insurance

- Traveling out of state or out of the country

- Gasoline if not brought back full

- Towing another vehicle or trailer

- Early pickup

- Late return

- Cleaning (inside and out)

- Damage

Never assume that anything is included in the rental price you've been quoted unless you are told that it is—in writing. When you read negative reviews of motorhome rentals, you will find that the overwhelming majority is due to being charged for something that the renter thought was included.

Unfortunately, this makes it very difficult to make price comparisons between RVs from two different sources. For example, I once rented a beautiful motorhome that had no mileage included in the base rental price. Instead, the dealer sold "mileage packages" of 500 miles each with a per-mile charge for any mileage over. Since the packaged miles were discounted from the per-mile fee, it made sense to buy as many as I thought I'd need, but none over what I'd actually drive, and figure that into the overall rental price. Other dealers or individuals may simply have a per-mileage fee that you pay when you return the coach, or give you 100 miles free for each day you rent with a mileage charge over that.

If you plan to do any boondocking (not camping in developed campgrounds, also known as dry camping or wilderness camping), you will need to factor in any extra hours you'll be running the generator. Some RVs come with three hours a day, some with none at all. To make it a bit easier, I've given you a price comparison chart (see below) that you can use to compare the various packages you may be offered.

Whenever possible, make an effort to talk with a live human being on the phone or visit the rental facility to take a first-hand look at the RVs. Get a feel for how they treat their customers and answer your questions. It's much easier to have a happy rental experience when you're dealing with friendly, helpful people.

Make sure that you understand what is and is not covered by your insurance, the owner's insurance, and any additional policy you may want or be required to buy. While some car insurance companies will cover you for liability while you're driving a rented RV, others will not. You need to confirm what is and isn't covered by your company and your policy. All of the chains and dealers will require you to purchase insurance against damage to their vehicle, or prove that you have that coverage through your own company. Usually these rental policies will have a $1,000 deductible, and the dealer will protect its liability by charging $1,000 against your credit card at the time of rental. You may also have the option of purchasing additional coverage. If you're renting from a private owner, you need to exercise even greater diligence to make sure that you have the insurance coverage you need. The following price comparison chart should help you organize all this information:

**Price Comparison Chart**

|  | Unit 1 | Unit 2 | Unit 3 | Unit 4 |
|---|---|---|---|---|
| **Base Price** | | | | |
| Estimated number of miles of travel | | | | |
| Miles included in base price | | | | |
| Expected miles beyond base (M) | | | | |
| Cost per mile above base (P) | | | | |
| **Total estimated mileage cost above base** **(M x P)** | | | | |
| Generator hours included in base | | | | |
| Estimated generator use (G) | | | | |
| Generator cost per hour over base (H) | | | | |

|  | Unit 1 | Unit 2 | Unit 3 | Unit 4 |
|---|---|---|---|---|
| Total estimated generator cost above base (G x H) |  |  |  |  |
| Pet Fee |  |  |  |  |
| Prep fee |  |  |  |  |
| Cleaning fee |  |  |  |  |
| Required Insurance |  |  |  |  |
| Supplemental Insurance |  |  |  |  |
| Linen Rental |  |  |  |  |
| Household Goods Rental |  |  |  |  |
| Propane Charge |  |  |  |  |
| Waste Tank Emptying Fee |  |  |  |  |
| Early Pickup Fee |  |  |  |  |
| Late Return Fee |  |  |  |  |

|  | Unit 1 | Unit 2 | Unit 3 | Unit 4 |
|---|---|---|---|---|
| **Bike Rack** |  |  |  |  |
| **Lawn Chairs** |  |  |  |  |
| **Child Booster Seat** |  |  |  |  |
| **GPS** |  |  |  |  |
| **Extra Driver fee** |  |  |  |  |
| **Airport Pickup/Dropoff Fee** |  |  |  |  |
| **Additional Fees** |  |  |  |  |
| **Tax** |  |  |  |  |
| **TOTAL** (All items in bold) |  |  |  |  |

(A printable version of this chart can be downloaded free at www.completervrentalguide.com)

So, now you've found a motorhome that's going to meet your needs for the kind of vacation you're planning, you're comfortable with the people you're dealing with, and you've read and understood the entire rental agreement. Congratulations! Pull out that credit card because it's time to put down a deposit and rent that RV!

# CHAPTER 3—DEFINING YOUR VACATION STYLE

You may already know exactly where you want to go, or perhaps you know the general area but not specifics. No matter what, here are some questions you should answer early in your planning.

Do you want to get away from it all, far from other human beings, and commune with nature? Or is your perfect vacation spot a major tourist destination with lots of shows, rides, and things to do? Are you thinking mountains, the beach, the desert, wine country, or the glaciers of Alaska? Would you like to visit the city, or live on a farm?

Are you starting your RV vacation close to home? Or will you be flying somewhere and picking up your RV at your destination? One advantage of starting at home is that you may be able to see the RV you're renting weeks or months before your vacation, and

you might choose to pick it up a day early so that you can pack all of your things the night before and leave first thing in the morning with a full day ahead of you. If you fly you'll have to trust the descriptions on a website, and you'll probably end up buying many of your supplies when you get there (unless you want to pay the airline to check a few extra bags). You'll probably pick up your RV in the afternoon, which means that you won't be able to (and shouldn't) drive very far the first day. On the other hand, we live in a large and beautiful country, and unless you have unlimited time (which most of us don't have on our vacations), flying is often the only way to get where you want to go.

Would you like to travel one way between two major destinations? Or would you be just as happy to navigate a circular route and end up where you began? One-way RV rentals are a great way to enjoy a dream itinerary such as San Francisco to Los Angeles, Maine to Florida, Chicago to New York, or getting your kicks on Route 66. But one-way rentals will definitely limit your rental options to national chains, and often come with a hefty premium unless you are going somewhere that the company needs to move extra vehicles. Renting round trip opens the world to rentals from local dealers and even private individuals who are trying to make a few dollars instead of letting their motorhome spend most of its time in their driveway.

While you're planning where you'd like to go, you need to be completely honest with yourself about how you like to travel. I know some people who measure the success of their vacation by the number of mornings they got to sleep in. These are usually folks who like to pick a spot and plant themselves, taking plenty of time to explore and enjoy the hidden gems of one or two locations. These are the people who like to "Stay and Play."

But I also know some folks who measure the success of their vacation by the number of miles they put on the odometer. They want to see as much as they can, and love that in their RV they can get up in the morning and hit the open road to their next destination. These are the people who like to "Drive and Seek."

The good news is that an RV is a great way to enjoy either of these styles of travel. With an RV you can find a hidden (and free) place to park on property owned by the Bureau of Land Management out West, or a spot nestled in a pineland forest in the East, and stay as long as your heart desires. The RV is your fully equipped home away from home, and if you get tired of a spot or don't like your neighbors, you can pull up stakes and move a few hundred yards or a few hundred miles. And if you feel like moving every day, you never have to unpack, make hotel reservations, or even go out to dinner. Your "vacation destination on wheels" will comfortably get you there and back while you enjoy the view from the road.

## Vacation Style Chart

| | |
|---|---|
| I want to be in the middle of the action | I want to get away from it all |
| I'll be staying close to home | I'll be flying |
| I'll pick up and drop off at the same place | I'll be driving one-way |
| I like to "drive and seek" | I like to "stay and play" |
| Five stars all the way | Just the basics – this is camping |

# CHAPTER 4—WHERE TO STAY

As a new RVer, you're probably going to spend most of your nights in campgrounds, and there are literally thousands to choose from—private, state, and national. Before choosing your specific campgrounds, here are several reasons to stay in campgrounds:

- Hookups—Most campgrounds provide a place for you to hook up your RV to get fresh drinking water for your faucets, electricity for your lights and appliances, and a destination for your liquid wastes (more on that in Chapter 9). If all three are provided, the campground is said to provide "full hookups." Partial hookups provide only one or two of the three utilities. There are also two levels of electric hookups: 30-amp and 50-amp. Most RVs under 30 feet are set up for 30-amp power, which is enough to run all of your basic appliances. But the bigger the rig, the more things there are onboard that use electricity. When you've got two or three air conditioners, a couple of big-screen TVs, house lights, computers, a coffee pot, and microwave/convection oven running, you're likely to need that 50-amp service. Some campgrounds charge extra for 50-amp service (after all, they are supplying you with more electricity), but the big RVs also have adapters for 30-amp service, and if you're not going to use all that energy, why pay more? (Learn about how to hook up in Chapter 9.)

• Security—Most campgrounds have some level of security, whether it's gates, security cameras, or a guard on duty during the night. And, since RVers tend to look out for one another, you've got a lot of eyes and ears nearby to notice and report anything out of the ordinary.

• Amenities—This is where campgrounds work hard to differentiate themselves from one another. The differences between campgrounds can be as dramatic as those between Motel 6 and the Ritz-Carlton. Typical amenities might include swimming pools (indoor or outdoor); Wi-Fi (free or paid); cable TV; a camp store with basic groceries and other supplies; a library; a full gym (or maybe just a treadmill and one stationary bike); laundry facilities; modern bathrooms and showers; a rec room with pool tables, Ping-Pong table, cards, puzzles, and a big screen TV; a pond stocked for fishing; shuttle service to local attractions, restaurants, or shopping; and bicycle rentals. You might even find a campground that offers a manager's cocktail reception.

• Activities—Not all campgrounds offer activities, but when they do they can range from access to a shuffleboard tournament to square dancing, family movie nights, tours, card games, and cooking classes. As a general rule, you're more likely to find scheduled and organized activities in one of the campground chains, but even some independents are more resort than just campground. Many state and national park campgrounds also offer activities centered around the appreciation of nature and history such as nature walks, lectures, and handicraft demonstrations.

- People—You may consider this a plus or a minus, but in most campgrounds you are going to be surrounded by other people. For many it's the socializing with the neighbors or gathering around a communal campfire that makes their vacation magical. And if you're new to RVing, it can be a big help to have some experienced campers around. Can't figure out how to back your RV into its space? Stand in the road scratching your head and pretty soon someone will come along and offer to help. Of course a few others will set up their lawn chairs to enjoy the free show! RVers tend to be a friendly bunch, so if you're sitting outside relaxing, someone's likely to stop by to say hello. And if you ask a couple of questions, they'll probably be happy to tell you some of their favorite stories from the road.

- Location—No matter how much you may enjoy being by yourself in a remote location, there are some places where the only place to park your RV is in a campground. I've stayed in a campground high on a bluff with a gorgeous view of the Pacific Ocean. I've also stayed in a crowded parking lot of RVs where I could barely open the door without hitting the next RV. But the campground was where I wanted to be (Pacifica, California) or needed to be (close to the airport).

- Cost—Independently run private campgrounds can vary in price from as low as $25/night to hundreds of dollars depending on the season, location, duration of your stay, and what they have to offer.

Now let's consider the types of campgrounds available.

---

## Private Campgrounds

Chances are you're going to spend some time in private campgrounds. Here are some ways you can find the private campgrounds that are right for you:

- Search the Good Sam Club (www.goodsamclub.com). In addition to the club's listing and ratings of RV parks all across the country, they have recently started to post camper reviews. You can purchase a printed copy of their travel guide, or download the free Good Sam Camping App for iOS or Android. Although Good Sam is a paid membership club (about $25 a year), these Internet resources are free for anyone to use. Members receive discounts at many listed parks, among other benefits. Even for the occasional RVer, the cost of membership can easily pay for itself through discounts on campsites and fuel.

• Check out the chains. The most famous campground chain is KOA (www.koa.com). With privately owned campgrounds across the country, the KOA franchise offers three kinds of campgrounds with different levels of amenities, depending on whether you just need a place to stay overnight or want to spend a few days in a fully equipped resort. For some families it's KOA or nothing! The much smaller Jellystone Park chain (www.campjellystone.com) caters to families with young kids, with lots of activities and daily visits by Yogi Bear.

The chains promise a consistent experience from park to park, but in fact the quality of individual campgrounds can vary widely. Both chains offer discount or rewards programs.

• Search www.reserveamerica.com for the region you will be traveling. In addition to being the reservation site for national parks and many state parks, this website can also help you find and book a site at many private campgrounds.

• Scan the listings and reviews on www.rvparkreviews.com. Organized by distance from a town or city you designate, these reviews are written by fellow campers to share the good, the bad, and the ugly of their experiences. As with any user review site, remember that one person's bad experience does not mean that the park is awful. Maybe the park, or the reviewer, was just having a bad day. Likewise, take glowing reviews with a grain of salt. They may have been written by the owner's family and friends!

- TripAdvisor (www.tripadvisor.com) has a limited number of campground reviews and is worth checking out if you aren't finding what you need in the above RV-specific websites.

- Google it. Run a search for RV parks in the area you'd like to visit. Sometimes you'll find a great park that's not listed in either of the big directories. Try the same thing on yelp.com.

- Check out the campground's webpage. This is where the owners will use words and pictures to give you the best possible impression of their campground and all they have to offer. A good website will have their rates clearly posted along with the campground's policies and restrictions (for instance "pet friendly," or "quiet hours after 10:00 p.m."). The website may allow you to make a reservation online, but most often they'll give you a phone number and/or an email address to make contact. Never forget that the website is designed to show the campground at its best, which means that pictures will be carefully cropped to eliminate any eyesores and present the best possible views of the scenery. In fact, in some cases photographs that appear to show views within the campground were actually taken miles away—which is why, in addition to looking at the campground's own website, you should...

• Map it. Google Maps (http://maps.google.com) has two great features that can give you an unbiased view of your potential campground. After entering the address of a campground, choose "Satellite View" to get a look at the property from above. You'll be able to see how close the sites are to one another, how many trees there actually are, and where the campground is located in relationship to major highways and railroad tracks. (For some reason, many campgrounds seem to be located right next to train tracks!) Google's "Street View" will also let you see what the park and neighborhood look like from street level.

• Ask around. The various online RV forums are a great resource to find out anything and everything RV, and no matter what you ask, someone is sure to have an opinion. Try the Good Sam forum at www.goodsamclub.com, the Escapees forum at www.rvnetwork.com, and the forum at www.iRV2.com.

- Check on YouTube. RVers love to share their camping experiences, and if you search for the area you'll be visiting or the name of a specific campground, you may just find a short video tour taken by a fellow traveler.

## State and National Parks

If you like a rustic setting, the first places you should consider are state and national parks. The cost is usually minimal, and the settings can be magnificent. The quality of the amenities can vary widely.

The place for one-stop shopping for National Park campgrounds is www.reserveamerica.com, which hosts the National Recreation Reservation Service (NRRS). The NRRS handles reservations for the US Forest Service, Army Corps of

Engineers, National Park Service, Bureau of Land Management, Bureau of Reclamation, Boundary Waters Canoe Area Wilderness, U.S. Fish and Wildlife Service, and National Archives & Records Administration.

Their website states, "With over 45,000 reservable facilities at over 1,700 locations, the NRRS is the largest outdoor recreation reservation service in the country. Whether you're heading North to Alaska's Tongass National Forest, South to Florida's Lake Okeechobee, East to North Carolina's Blue Ridge Parkway, or West to California's Los Padres National Forest, you can reserve your place under the stars with the NRRS." There you'll find several nice features: the opportunity to create an account so you only have to set up your personal information once; interactive maps of the campsites that list the maximum size rig each site can handle; each site's hookups; and which spaces are available. In other words, you can reserve the particular campsite where you'll stay.

You can find information about national parks that do not accept reservations at www.nps.gov.

Reserve America also handles campground reservations for many states, so you're in luck if that includes the states you are visiting. Otherwise Google "[Name of State] State Park Camping Reservations."

## Speaking of Reservations

Should you reserve campsites before you start your vacation? By now you can probably guess the answer to that question: it depends.

A rule of thumb is that the more rustic the campground, the more likely that they will have limited spaces available for large (over 32 feet) motorhomes. So if you want to get away from it all but also have all the comforts of a large coach, I recommend that you reserve your spots ahead of time.

Reservations are always a good idea for holiday weeks or weekends, and the further ahead you can book your spot, the better. There will be lots of other folks out there competing with you for that limited resource.

Whenever possible, I like to book ahead for state and national parks as well, especially during their high season. These parks can fill up fast—and the more popular the park, the earlier it will fill. You can make reservations at most national parks as early as six months in advance. Yosemite is an exception so check their website for when the reservation window opens for the specific days you'd like to be there.

One nice thing about most popular national parks is that, in addition to their own campground, there are usually a number of private campgrounds just outside of the park border. So, if you can't get a spot in the park itself, search nearby for what may be a great alternative.

No matter the campground or season, it's always wise to call ahead to make a reservation—even on the same day if you expect to arrive after their office closes, which is often as early as 5:00 p.m. Remember that the bigger your rig, the more limited the number of spaces available. Keep that in mind and plan ahead. Calling even a few hours before your arrival is always a good idea. It will assure that you don't end a long day of driving by pulling into a campground that's already full or closed for the day. Most campgrounds have a late check-in system that will allow you to pick up whatever you need and drive right to your assigned spot long after the office closes—but only if you've called ahead.

If having a fixed itinerary with every night planned in advance gives you peace, go ahead and reserve. One caveat is that you will also have to make deposits on your reservations that are often not refundable. If you want to stay at a campground longer than planned because you've discovered a "hidden gem" of a location, you might mess up your original reservations and itinerary and lose some deposit money.

That's one reason why most long-time RVers prefer flexibility to predictability and make reservations only at major destinations, favorite RV parks, and on the first and last nights of their vacation. Reservations on the first night are handy because you'll probably be picking up your rental RV late in the afternoon and shouldn't plan to drive very far. And even experienced RVers prefer to arrive at their destination before dark so that they can set up at leisure. On the last night you'll want to make a reservation close to where you need to return the RV. Most rental places expect you to check in fairly early—and the check-in process itself can take as long as an hour, with paperwork, unloading your belongings, and an inspection of the RV. It's nice to avoid the stress of looking for that last overnight spot on your very last day.

Of course, reservations aren't an issue if you're . . .

## Boondocking

Boondocking (also known as dry camping, wild camping, or wilderness camping) is parking your RV on private or public land without any hookups. The subject of boondocking is extensive enough to warrant a book of its own, but this will be enough to get you going if boondocking is your style.

The two major styles of boondocking are asphalt and wilderness.

**Asphalt boondocking** is a great way to save money when all you need is a place to park your rig and fall asleep. The most popular sites for overnight boondocking are the parking lots of Wal-Mart, Home Depot, Cracker Barrel, Costco, and other RV-friendly stores. You can also boondock at some highway rest areas along with the truckers. The advantages are obvious: you will generally be in lighted parking lots with security cameras and guards, and it's free.

When asphalt boondocking, there are some important points of etiquette that you should follow, both for your sake and for future RVers who need a free place to stay:

•  Always ask permission before setting up for overnight. If the business is open, go in and speak to the manager. If it's closed, look for a security person or car on patrol. Wouldn't you hate to have that same guard (or the police) come knocking on your door at 1:00 in the morning asking you what you're doing there and telling you to move along?

• If it's a business, buy something. If it's a restaurant, eat something. Doing so leaves a good impression and increases the likelihood that they'll say yes to the next RVer who comes along, too.

• Keep your slides and awnings in, if you have them, and don't even think about setting up your lawn chairs and grill to cook, eat, or sit outside. Don't think of this as a campground. Think of it as a place to sleep for the night.

• Stay only one night. Again, it's not a campground.

• In the morning haul out your trash (don't "borrow" the business's dumpster unless specifically invited to do so), go inside to thank the owner/manager, and do your best to leave no footprint as you drive away.

**Wilderness boondocking** is entirely different, of course. In the United States, many local, state, and national parks have wilderness sites that will accommodate an RV, and the cost is usually just a couple of bucks a night. In the Western U.S. vast parcels of land are owned and managed by the U.S. Bureau of Land Management (www.blm.gov). Many have designated areas where you can camp for as long as a week at no charge, surrounded by the most magnificent scenery the nation has to offer. You can download a handy app for Apple or Android devices called U.S. Public Lands that shows you a map of all U.S. public lands with links to the websites that manage each property (http://www.twostepsbeyond.com/apps/uspubliclands/).

Finally, for $25 a year you can join www.boondockerswelcome.com, a site that connects you with private families that will be pleased to allow you to park for free on their land!

So, how do you get along for a night (or two or three) without hookups? The good news is that your rental RV will have a large fresh-water tank that you can fill. It should provide you with all the water you need for a couple of days (assuming you don't take long showers in those tiny RV shower stalls). For electricity your RV will have one or more "house" batteries that get charged while you are driving and provide for your lights, water pump, and other low-level electrical needs. You'll also probably have a generator (which you may or may not have to pay for by the hour) that you can run when you need the air conditioner or microwave.

For heat, cooking, and refrigeration you'll be carrying propane. The refrigerator in most rental motorhomes will be a special small RV fridge that runs on either electricity or propane. Many manufacturers are now including residential-sized electric refrigerators in their larger RVs, which means that you'll need more battery power to keep them running without hookups.

As for sewage, you've got two tanks on board, one for "gray" water (dirty water from your sinks or shower), and another for "black" water, which collects everything you flush down the toilet.

If you're planning to do only an occasional night of boondocking, most motorhomes will get you through. But if you're hoping to spend multiple days and nights in the wilderness, you'll need to check with the agent or owner to see if the house batteries, fresh water tank, and holding tanks have the capacity you'll need. A growing trend is for motorhomes to have solar panels to recharge the house batteries and run your appliances, but these are only available in the highest-level rental units or rentals directly from owners.

In other words, be sure to choose a rental RV that will be adequate to meet your needs and suitable for the type of places you'll want to visit!

# CHAPTER 5—PLANNING YOUR ITINERARY

Now that you know what kind of RV you'll be driving and what kind of campground you're looking for, it's time to plan your specific itinerary. Of course you've probably started your planning already, but here are some tips to make your journey as fun and stress-free as possible. It's not as easy as it might first sound, with many things to consider: route, travel time, attractions along the way, where to stay, and for how long.

The most important advice that I can give for planning your itinerary for an RV vacation is: "Take it easy, and take your time."

## Choosing Your Route

By now you know generally where you want to go. "I want to see the California Coast," "We want to drive the Blue Ridge Parkway," or "Florida, here we come!" Next, start making a list of all of the things you'd like to see and do while you're there. Search websites such as TripAdvisor (www.tripadvisor.com) to get recommendations for activities, historical sites, local walking tours, sights to see, and more. Go to the state's tourism website to get a sense of what's different or popular and discover whether there are any special events or festivals that you might enjoy. One of my favorite places to get help with itinerary ideas is the "Good Sam Open Roads Forum" under the topic "Roads and Routes." You'll find lots of experienced RVers with advice and opinions about what you should do and where you should go. Of course, with this and similar forums, you should "take what you like, and leave the rest."

After you have a comprehensive list of things to do and places to go, it's time to cut that list in half, and probably in half again! You can't do it all, and if you try, you'll find that the confines of a small motorhome are great at amplifying stress and conflict. You're on vacation, so "take it easy and take your time." Cut your list down to no more than one or two planned activities each day (and yes, driving 100 miles is a "planned activity"). Leave plenty of free time to sleep in, walk on the beach, grill hamburger and hot dogs over a campfire, go out for a nice dinner, watch a video with your kids, listen to the sounds of nature, and go to bed early.

At this point I suggest that you go back to the Good Sam website (www.goodsamclub.com) and take advantage of their free trip planner. This wonderful online tool lets you plot out the route you'd like to travel by entering the places you want to visit and where you'd like to stay along the way. Not only will the map help you plan your route and warn you of RV-unfriendly roads; it will also show you campgrounds near your route, sights you might want to see, and how long it will take to get from one place to another. It's great for playing "what if" when planning your itinerary. "What if I don't go to the Bottle Cap Museum?" "What if I take back roads instead of the highway?" "What if I spend two nights here instead of only one?"

I like to plot my itinerary over the course of several days or even weeks. Sometimes I'll go back and ask follow-up questions in a forum, and of course I'll talk about our options with my wife and teenagers. Reading and thinking about the places you'll be going not only helps you prioritize your time. It's also part of the fun!

Whenever possible, I prefer to drive no more than four hours in a day. Still, it seems like I always have one marathon day where I just have to drive for six to eight hours to get from point A to point B. On those occasions, one of the great advantages of an RV is that people can spread out a bit, nap, play cards at the table, and read or watch videos. Plus, your own bathroom is only a few steps away!

Remember though, despite the fact that it's possible for your passengers to get up, walk around, make themselves a snack in the kitchen, and use the bathroom, seat belts are located throughout the motorhome for a reason. Think how far a body could fly if you had to make a sudden stop or swerve while traveling at full speed down the highway. If someone needs to get up, go ahead and pull over to the side for a couple of minutes. Better to be safe than early!

# CHAPTER 6—PACKING

After you've got everything planned, there are several factors to take into account as you prepare to pack for your RV vacation. The most important, of course, is your destination and the time of year. But let's look at some additional things you might need to consider.

If you are driving to pick up your rental unit, it's easy to bring along just about anything you want. If you're heading to the beach, you can haul along the beach chairs, umbrella, towels, and even a surfboard. Love grilling? You can easily pack a compact grill in the storage area of most RVs. You may want to bring along a folding table for picnics when there isn't one available at your campsite. At a minimum you'll want to bring along some folding chairs so that you can sit outside and enjoy the sunset while sipping your favorite beverage, and linens so that you don't have to pay a hefty fee to rent a "convenience kit" from the dealer. If you're renting from a place that charges extra for pots and pans, cooking utensils, dishes and cups, you should definitely bring those along as well. We've learned to bring or buy paper plates, cups, and so on for our trips. Despite being environmentally conscientious, we've learned that the less dish washing we have to do on vacation, the better!

If you're flying, you will be able to bring only the essentials and will have to decide whether it's worth the baggage fees for an extra suitcase or two. One thing we've learned to bring along, even if it means paying for an extra suitcase, is blankets, sheets, and towels. Renting linens from the dealer can cost upwards of $55 <u>per person</u> for your vacation (so for our family of five, that's $275)! Consider that against paying for one extra suitcase on most airlines, and you may want to fit linens for your whole family in one large suitcase. On the other hand, it's probably worth your while to rent camp chairs along with your RV if they are available, since packing them could be a challenge.

Regardless of how you're getting to your motorhome, there are a few other special items you should consider when packing.

## What to Bring

• Rubber Gloves—You're going to want these for when you hook and unhook the sewage hose. My experience is that the discharge valves on many rental units are somewhat less than fully functional. With one unit we rented, fluid from the black-water tank (potty tank) poured out on me every time I unscrewed the cover to hook up the sewer hose. Yuck! Don't go for lightweight latex gloves such as those found in the doctor's office. They rip easily and are hard to pull on and off. I recommend "Thickster" gloves, available on Amazon.

• Flashlight—Bring a powerful one. Despite your best planning, you may need to work on your hookups after dark. Do you really want to hold onto your cell phone flashlight while you're doing that? Plus, a large flashlight can come in handy for navigating to the shower house at night in an unfamiliar campground.

• GPS—We use an iPad as our GPS while driving an RV. It has a nice big screen (unlike a regular phone), and you can get mounts that allow you to attach it to the windshield. If you have a dedicated GPS unit that has up-to-date maps, that will work well also. If you are using your tablet or cell phone, you might consider installing a truck GPS app that will help you avoid low bridges or roads best not traveled by anything as large as a motorhome. I haven't found a need for one of these yet, but many RVers swear by them.

• Toiletry Items—We all have our favorite brands, and they are light and easy to throw into the suitcase. The same for bug spray, sunscreen, etc. You can of course purchase these along the way, but save your money and take with you whatever you can. Storage areas in the RV bathrooms vary, but so far they've been sufficient for our family of five on a weeklong vacation.

• Clothing—Pack for any kind of weather you're likely to encounter. But don't overpack! Chances are you won't feel the need to change clothes as often as you would on a hotel vacation.

• Games—Having a deck of cards or a few board games can be a great way to bring the family together in the evening, or reduce the monotony of a long drive for your passengers.

• Chargers—For all of your electronics. Bring both 120-volt chargers that plug into a regular wall outlet, and a couple of 12-volt chargers that plug into a cigarette lighter. A few long charging cords will be helpful as well.

• Sharp Knives—I say this as someone who loves to cook. The rental knives are almost always horribly dull. It's easy to pack two or three knives and bring them along (NOT in your carry-on if you're flying!).

• Binoculars—To get closer views of the wildlife you'll see along the way.

• Medications—Make sure you have enough for a few extra days in case you encounter unforeseen delays during your travels.

• A copy of your rental agreement.

• Extension Cords—They will save you a lot of frustration when an outlet is just out of reach for one of your appliances—or multiple appliances. Bring along one or two power strips, too. If nothing else, you'll find they are convenient for plugging in the chargers for your electronics.

• A Sharpie pen—For writing names on plastic cups, etc.

• Screwdrivers (Flat Head and Phillips) and an adjustable wrench—It's not your job to make repairs on someone else's motorhome, but a couple of tools can be helpful for anything from loosening a hose fitting to tightening the handle on a cabinet.

• Duct Tape—Because it comes in handy for just about everything!

## What to Buy on the Road

We've found that it's always a good idea to make a grocery store and/or dollar store your first stop after picking up your motorhome. You'll need to stock up on things that made no sense to pack. And if you're far from home, you'll find that this is your first chance to get a taste of the local culture. Besides, after the stress of driving or flying and picking up the RV (see Chapter 7), it's a great opportunity to buy yourself a little treat to really get the vacation started.

• Food Items—Unless you have special dietary needs that will make it difficult for you to buy food where you're traveling, it's usually best to buy what you need after you pick up your RV. We've discovered that some rental units will leave on board things such as dish detergent, a few spices, and other condiments used by previous renters.

(You might also find these free for the taking in the RV rental office.) Make a list of meals and snacks you expect to have in the first day or two and buy them at a local store. You'll quickly get a better sense of what will fit in the refrigerator and what other items you need to buy.

• Kitchen Utensils (if you're not renting them)—You can often buy cheap kitchen tools (even pots and pans) at a discount store for less than the cost of renting them. If you don't want to carry them home with you, you can donate them to the local Goodwill or Salvation Army.

• Trash Bags—If you're buying groceries, the plastic bags you get at checkout can serve double duty as trash bags. (We discovered that plastic bags are banned in California, however, and were caught by surprise when store after store used only paper bags.)

• Disposable Food Containers—Use them for the duration of the trip, then toss before you head home.

This is also an opportunity to pick up the duct tape, sunglasses, batteries, etc. that you forgot to pack (see above), some campfire supplies, and so on. These lists are not comprehensive, but they should help you cover the basics.

# CHAPTER 7—PICKING UP YOUR RV

This is the moment you've been waiting for! You are pulling into the RV dealer's parking lot, or perhaps meeting someone at a shopping center to pick up your rental RV. It's also an important time to pay attention to details so that you can make the most of your vacation.

Be prepared to fill out a pile of paperwork! If you boil it all down, you're signing documents that make you fully responsible for anything and everything that happens while you have possession of the RV, and relieves the owner of liability for anything.

Pay careful attention to be sure that the terms you were given in advance are actually the terms on the paperwork you are signing. Check to be sure the insurance is what you agreed to. Make note of the date and time you are to return the vehicle, and what condition they expect it to be in. If you are expected to return it with tanks empty, ask where the nearest dump station is in case you aren't able to empty the tanks in a campground that morning. If anything needs to be changed in the contract, discuss it, have it written on the contract itself, initial it, and have the owner initial the change also. If it's not in writing, it's not enforceable.

You are about to take possession of a vehicle that is probably worth anywhere from $50,000 to $500,000! It is in both your and the owner's interests to make sure there are no misunderstandings before you hand over your credit card or write that big rental check and they hand over their RV.

The next important part of picking up your motorhome is the pre-departure tour and inspection. You should expect this to take as much as an hour.

Starting on the inside of the RV, the owner should give you a thorough explanation and demonstration of every system, including the ones you think you understand. If something has a switch, turn it on to be sure it works. Some of the things that they should demonstrate inside the RV include the propane level indicator; black, gray, and fresh water levels; water heater; refrigerator; air conditioner and furnace; toilet (including instructions on any kind of chemicals they want you to use); microwave and stove; entertainment system; roof vents; power steps; opening and closing each of the beds; adjusting the cab chairs; and locating the seat belts for every passenger seat. Find out where all manuals are stored (each accessory has its own) for reference during your vacation.

On the outside of the motorhome, do a thorough inspection for damage—no matter how small—and record it. The owner should open every hatch and explain the workings of every piece of equipment. Learn how to roll out the awning. Find out where the fresh-water hose is stored, as well as the sewage hose, and how to hook both of them up (see Chapter 9). Check the electrical system, and if it is a 50-amp system, make sure you are provided an adapter for 30-amp service. Look under the hood and check the fluid levels. Confirm that the fuel tank is full. You will probably not be allowed to climb onto the roof, but if you can, ask to take a picture from the ladder as a record of the pre-rental condition. Do you really want to pay to replace an antenna that was already broken?

**If something can be opened, open it.**

**If it can be closed, close it.**

**If you don't understand it,**

**ask them to show you again.**

You're going to be taking in a lot of information in a short period of time. If you have the ability to do so, I suggest that you or your traveling companion take a video of the entire inspection and tour. When you find something that is scratched, dented, bent, cracked, loose, or in any way damaged, point it out, see that it gets written down, and take a picture so that there will be no disputes when you return the vehicle. Even if something is simply dirty, make a note of it.

If you've got older kids with you, they should have finished loading all the luggage while you've been doing this, right? All right! You're ready to hit the open road—as long as you've done your driving homework!

# CHAPTER 8—DRIVING

Driving an RV is like driving a truck or bus. It is heavy, makes wide turns, gets blown around in the wind, and has no center rearview mirror. No matter how prepared you are, it will take a while to get a sense of where you are in relation to the sides of the road.

This is the point in the book where I could give you detailed written instructions on how to safely drive a motorhome. I'll give you a few. But before I do that, I urge you to set aside an hour or so and watch "The New RV Driver Confidence Course" with Barney Alexander produced by Lazydays. It's free. The direct YouTube link is https://youtu.be/4CeThR_A4VI but it's probably easier to just go to www.youtube.com and search for this 42-minute video by name. If you'll be driving with a partner, have that person sit down and watch the video with you. Barney Alexander teaches what you need to know to drive safely and with confidence, covering everything from adjusting the mirrors, knowing your blind spots, making turns and going around tight curves in the road, and (gulp) backing into a campsite!

Is this video a little repetitive? Yes. Will you be glad you watched it? Yes! So before you read any further, it's time to take a break and watch the video. Really. Watch the video!

Great! Now let me highlight some of the most important principles:

• Swing wide and go slowly around corners. You don't want to bring a stop sign home with you.

• Never back up your motorhome without a spotter on the outside to guide you. Never. Never ever! Not even just a few feet. Agree to specific hand signals your spotter will use to direct you, and never back up if you can't see your spotter in the mirror.

• Your mirrors are your best friends. Get them adjusted properly before you start driving.

• Know your blind spots.

My wife and I watched this video together before heading out for the first time in a 31-foot Class A motorhome, and we paid special attention to the "3 and 1 system" for backing into a campsite. It's a good thing we did, because on our third night out, we pulled into our campground and discovered that every one of their campsites required us to back the RV in. (For the first two nights, I'd managed to snag a pull-through.) My hands got so sweaty that I could hardly hold onto the wheel. But we stuck to the system we had learned from Barney. We had already marked a spot eight feet ahead of the rear wheels on each side of the coach, and we surveyed the site to be aware of any obstacles or tree branches we needed to avoid. Then we held our breath and tried the system.

- Start with the entrance of the campsite on the left side with the motorhome about two feet from the left side of the road, and the spotter standing in front of the campsite about a foot-and-a-half before the far end of the site an arm's length from the coach. Pull forward until the spotter is even with the driver's window. This is position one.

- Pull straight forward until the spotter is eight feet in front of the rear wheels (the position you already marked). This is position two.

- Turn the wheel as far right as it can go, and pull forward just until you can no longer see the spotter's right shoulder in the mirror. This is position three.

- Now turn the wheel all the way to the left, and with the spotter moving backward into the campsite, back up the motorhome, always keeping the spotter in view in your mirror. When the RV is lined up straight within the campsite, straighten the wheels and follow the spotter's directions to back in until the hookups on your RV (they are on the driver's side) are even with the campground utility attachments.

- Place the RV into "park," turn off the ignition, and get out to admire your handiwork!

Does this sound ridiculously complicated? It's very clear when you watch the animation on the video. You did watch the video, didn't you? I'm pleased to say that we successfully parked our RV on our first attempt, and we continue to use this system whenever we are on the road. If you don't have a partner with you, recruit another camper to help you. Then, after you're parked, set out your lawn chairs and enjoy watching how other RVers back into their sites.

Here are a few more tips:

• Write down the clearance height of the motorhome and keep it on your dashboard. Always check the clearance on bridges and overpasses off the main highway before proceeding. And be sure to check the overhead clearance at gas stations before pulling through.

• Before you enter a parking lot, think through how you are going to exit. You want to park as far from other vehicles as possible to allow maximum room for maneuvering, usually along the outside edge of the lot. If you do have to park in marked spaces, take four parking spaces with your rig smartly in the middle. No matter how much care you take, sooner or later someone's going to park too close and block your exit. Aren't you glad you've got a nice comfortable motorhome to sit in while you wait for them to leave?

• Call ahead to get instructions for RV parking whenever you are going to an attraction or event. On a recent trip to California we wanted to visit a fun "tourist trap" just off of Highway 1 along the coast. Fortunately we called ahead and learned that there is a one-lane road into and out of the attraction, and were told to call again when we reached the turnoff. These nice folks had already marked out a spot for our rig in the parking lot before our arrival, and stopped outbound traffic as we navigated our way up the road—a good start for an enjoyable and fun couple of hours!

• Take your time. RVing isn't a marathon. Whenever possible, don't plan on driving more than a few hours each day. And while you're driving, take it slow. Your rig will likely get less than ten miles per gallon. It's not only more relaxing but also a lot more economical to keep the speed at 55 mph or less. RVs are not particularly aerodynamic, and going from 55 to 75 mph can result in a 40% to 50% reduction in miles per gallon. In other words, if you're getting 10 mpg at 55, you'll be getting closer to 5.5 to 6 mpg at 75. Use the cruise control on highways. Edmunds.com found that using cruise control can save up to 7% compared to regulating your speed manually on the highway. With (almost) all the comforts of home in your RV, why rush?

• If traveling with a partner, and that partner is willing, both of you should be able to drive your motorhome, even if one of you is the primary driver. If you get weary or even ill, your partner can take over. Practice in a parking lot, drive in the slow lane, and be supportive and encouraging. And watch that video together, multiple times! (Have I said to watch the video enough times?)

Of course this vacation is not just about driving. It's also about camping. So let's talk about what to do after you pull into your campsite.

# CHAPTER 9—AT THE CAMPGROUND

You made it! You've arrived at your first campground with your rental RV. And I hope you've come early enough to have plenty of daylight to park, hook up, and settle in. If you've made it this far, the rest should be easy and fun. And yes, this is the chapter where we will talk about the dreaded poop!

---

## Arrival

After pulling through the gate into the campground, your first job is to find the office, which is usually, but not always, just inside the gate. So either pull your RV to the area designated for check in, or if there isn't one, find a place to pull to the side, out of the way of traffic. Since you've called ahead, you already know there's a space waiting for you (you did call ahead, didn't you?) and it's time to check in and find out where you'll be parking.

The first few times driving an RV, I always requested a pull-through site when making our reservation or calling ahead. If there are a limited number of pull-throughs, they are usually set aside for trailers or really big motorhomes, but I was never ashamed to say loud and clear that I was a newbie and to ask for the easiest access site they had.

Now this can lead to one of two responses from the management. A rare few campground hosts have a twisted sense of humor and haven't had much entertainment lately, so they will assign you a back-in site that's just barely big enough for your rig! But upon hearing that you're a newbie, most hosts will have a horrific vision of you trying to back into one of their sites, clipping into their hookups and flattening them to the ground, and felling a tree or two along the way. Not wanting to risk damage to their property or add to their ever-growing list of chores, chances are they'll assign you a nice big space with plenty of room to maneuver.

Depending on the size of the campground and its level of luxury, you may either receive a map to your site or be escorted by a campground host (perhaps on an electric golf cart). Take it easy now, you can do this!

When you get to the site, put the rig into "park" and get out to survey the situation. Look above and to the sides to see if there are any tree branches or other obstacles you want to avoid when pulling in and also when extending your slide(s). If you have slides, your RV will be several feet wider at rest than it is on the road, and many campgrounds have nice wide sites with plenty of space between you and your neighbors. But sometimes your slides and your neighbor's slides may become kissing cousins. (You did take a satellite view of the campground before making your reservation to check this out, right?)

Assuming the way is clear, it's time to pull in. Follow Barney's instructions (see Chapter 8) and you'll be fine. Even if you have a pull-through, it's best to have your traveling companion or the campground host direct you as you position your rig. You have two goals here: 1) Don't hit anything; and 2) Position yourself for the most convenient access to the hookups. As mentioned before, the hookup connections on your motorhome will usually be located in one of the hatches on the driver's side of the rig.

The water hose and electrical cord that came with the motorhome are probably both long enough to reach wherever you need. The sewer hose, however, often is not. I don't know why they do it, but more often than not these rental units have the cheapest, shortest sewer hoses available, and I promise you, even though it's made of corrugated plastic that looks like the bellows of an accordion, you do not want to have to stretch that thing in order to reach the dump pipe. Park so that your sewage connections are as close to the campsite's dump pipe (usually a capped white PVC pipe flush with the ground) as possible.

## Hooking Up

Once you're parked, it's time to connect your hookups. The good news is that the easiest utilities to hook up are the ones you're going to need first. I'm assuming you're at a campground with full hookups. You might want to just skim these instructions until a few hours before you need to actually do it all. You should have also had a review of how to hook up everything from your rental company or owner. But here are the details on how to hook up your RV for the night.

## Electric

First, inside one of the compartments on the outside of your RV you will find a heavy-duty electrical cord. At the side of the campsite, you'll find a closed electrical box mounted on a low pole. When you open the front panel of the box you'll often see two (sometimes three) outlets where you can plug in. How do you know which one to use? Whichever one fits the plug on the end of your cord! If none of them fits, it means that you have an RV set up for s-amp service but you're parked in a 30-amp site (which is the most common). Don't worry. Check again and you'll probably find an adapter plug that will allow you to hook in to the lower service. The only downside is that you won't be able to run quite as many electrical appliances at the same time. (If that's a problem, you can request a 50-amp site, which will usually cost a few dollars more each night because of the extra power you're likely to use.) You'll also see a couple of circuit breakers in the box. Plug in your cord, then flip on the corresponding breaker, and now you've got "shore power" (from grid rather you're your generator) throughout the rig!

## Water

Even though your RV has a built-in tank of water for washing and drinking, you'll almost certainly want to hook up to the park's water supply. To use the water you're carrying requires that it be pumped out of the tank, and the rattle of the pump whenever you open a faucet can get annoying. And, as a matter of preference, I'd just rather drink water piped from a well or the city water system than water that's been sloshing around for who knows how long in a big plastic tank in someone else's RV.

In another compartment outside of the RV, you'll find a hose that's specifically certified for carrying drinking water. Usually these hoses are white, although occasionally they may be blue. Hopefully it hasn't been stored in the same compartment that holds the outlets from the black and gray-water tanks. If it has, I'd be inclined to head into the camp store and invest in a new hose just for the peace of mind it will bring, or at a minimum wipe down the hose fittings with a disinfectant.

Here's a tip: Cover the ends of your water hose with plastic bags secured by rubber bands or twisties when storing in order to keep out sand and dirt.

I prefer to connect the shore end of the water hose first. This way, before connecting to the RV I can open the valve and let some clean water flow through the hose to flush out any debris and clear any air pockets. Then, keeping the open end of the hose clear of the ground, I connect to the threaded city water input on the side of the RV. Be sure the RV's water pump is off, and then turn on the outside faucet to have fresh running water.

## Dumping Your Gray and Black Tanks

You only need to hook up the sewage connections at your site when you're actually planning to dump the tanks (when either one is two-thirds or more full). If you're planning to use your RV for local travel, hooking and unhooking the sewer hose each time you leave the site will quickly become discouraging. Besides, you won't want (or need) to dump your gray and black tanks any more often than you have to! If the tanks are not at least two-thirds full, leave them alone. If one is at the two-thirds mark and the other is not, open some sink faucets to fill (but not overfill) the gray-water tank, and hold down the toilet flusher to fill (but not overfill) the black-water tank. Then turn off the faucets and head outside.

Why fill the tanks before emptying them? To put this as delicately as possible, the chunky stuff that goes into your black-water tank will not flow through that sewer hose unless there's enough water pressure to push it along. This is why you don't want to empty the black-water tank until it is at least half, and preferably two-thirds, full.

As mentioned earlier, your RV has two tanks for waste water. The gray-water tank is connected to the drains in the kitchen sink, bathroom sink, and shower. The black-water tank is connected to the toilet. The drains for both tanks come together in a "Y" fitting in one of the compartments outside of your RV. Each tank has its own individual shut-off valve to allow flow to the one connection where you will attach the sewage hose.

Now is the time you want to put on those rubber gloves you packed. Yes, you can do this barehanded, but do you really want to?

Before unscrewing the cap from the end of the drain on the RV, double-check to be sure that the valves to both the gray and black-water tanks are completely closed. These will be gate valves, which means that you'll push a handle in toward the RV to close, and pull it out to open. Sometimes this takes a bit of strength due to corrosion or built-up crud. Seriously, you don't want either of these tanks draining out all over you and onto the ground. Make sure they are closed!

If the valves are functioning smoothly and closing tightly, nary a drop of fluid will land on your hands when you take the end cap off of the sewage connection. If not, well, that's what the gloves are for.

Most sewer hoses connect to the RV using a bayonet connection. Push the end of the hose onto the outlet, and then turn it to the right about a quarter turn until it stops and is securely attached. If you pull on it, there should be no wobble. Leave the tank valves CLOSED.

Open the cap on the campground's sewage input, and carefully stretch your sewer hose to the opening and place it in. Most sewer hoses will have a solid plastic male connecter on the end that will fit nicely into the pipe and perhaps even screw in. Unfortunately, many sewer hoses or sewer pipes don't have the option of a screw-on fitting. Now, have you noticed that hunk of concrete block or the big rock sitting on the ground next to the hookups? I'd like you to imagine what will happen to the end of your hose when you open the -s and release the pressure of fifty gallons of dirty water from the RV. Yep, just like a rocket engine it will shoot itself out of the campground's fitting and begin to pour its sloshy soup all over the place, making you and your neighbors very unhappy campers. The rock is there to rest on top of the hose to hold it in when the effluent starts flowing. If possible, have a companion at the other end of the hose to assure that it doesn't shoot out of the ground despite your careful rock placement.

Step 1: Pull open only the gray-water tank valve.

Here's what you want to happen: The gray water dumps through the valve, flows evenly through your sewage hose, and gently down into the ground; then you close the valve and refill the tank for step three.

Here's what probably will happen: The gray water will dump through the valve, but because the ground is lower than the input to the camp's sewer pipe most of the water will just flow into the hose and sit there. Most of campers who own their own rigs have some kind of hose support system to raise the sewer hose off the ground so that gravity can take its course. But since you don't want to make that kind of investment for a motorhome you don't own, all you need to do is lift the hose off the ground starting close to your RV and, working toward the outlet, move the fluid down the hose and into the sewer hole. This is not that gross to do unless . . .

Here's what could happen: The gray water dumps through the valve and starts squirting like a water fountain through tiny invisible cracks and holes in the sewage hose, before shooting the end of the hose out of the ground and all over your companion who wasn't really paying attention! Now, aren't you glad you did this with fresh water instead of what's in the black-water tank?

If you discover leaks in the sewage hose, go into the camp store and buy a new one—the longest one they have—and keep the receipt to be reimbursed when you return the RV. If there is no camp store or it's not open (they often close by 5 or 6 p.m.—another reason to plan to arrive early at your campgrounds), close the gray-water tank valve, take off your sewer hose, screw the caps back onto the RV and campground pipes, and be glad that you still have room in the tanks to get you through the night (or even a couple of nights if you have to).

Assuming that you didn't have any leaks, you should now close the valve to the gray-water tank then go inside and refill the gray-water tank at least 2/3 full.

Step 2: Check again to be sure that your sewer hose is firmly seated in the campground drainpipe and solidly connected to the drainpipe on the RV. Again, if possible, have someone hold the hose firmly into the campground drain. (Go ahead and splurge. Give them a pair of gloves too!) Now fully open the gate to let the black-water tank discharge into the hose. (Did your sewer hose come with a clear plastic connecter? Isn't that pleasant!)

Once the black-water tank is fully drained, close the valve. If there's a lot of fluid accumulated in the hose, carefully lift the hose to pour it down the drain. You probably won't be able to get it all, which is why you'll be glad that you emptied the black water first.

Step 3: Now, firmly and fully open the valve from the gray-water tank. Smile as all of that gray water flushes through the hose and into the ground, carrying any leftovers from the black-water tank with it. When the gurgling stops, close the valve.

If you want to be really thorough, at this point could you could go back into the RV, refill the two tanks with clean water from the faucets, and flush them again. But really, this is your vacation, so unless it looks particularly nasty, there's no reason to do so. I certainly haven't!

There. That wasn't so bad, was it?

# Wi-Fi

When my wife and I travel with our teenagers, being away from the Internet for too long a period of time can result in minor grumpiness or major complaints. Although we have a data plan for our mobile phones, it's easy to eat up a full month's worth of expensive data in just a couple of days if it's being used to send video clips to friends, watch YouTube, or play online games. I know that purists will say that bringing along personal electronics is contrary to the values of camping. Hey, if that's your thing, go for it! But in our case we've found that the ability to connect can keep the kids happy and make the vacation a better experience for us all. And that's our goal!

Many campgrounds advertise that they provide free Wi-Fi. I remember being excited as we pulled into a beautiful site and saw their free Wi-Fi network on my laptop. "This is great!" I thought. "Let's go on Netflix and have a family movie night." I couldn't have been more wrong. The further we were from the clubhouse, the weaker the Wi-Fi, and to tell the truth it wasn't even very good there. "We're out in the country," the hostess explained. "This is pretty much the best we can get." Having given up on streaming Netflix, I decided to take my laptop into the clubhouse and download a movie on Amazon. Visions of watching RV with the kids and laughing at Robin Williams' misadventures danced in my head. Well, eventually we did get to watch the movie—but it took about five hours to download!

The point is that you should take advertisements of "Free High-Speed Internet" with a hefty grain of salt.

## Cable

Many campgrounds also provide cable TV, either free or at a nominal charge. Hey, why does camping mean that you have to miss the big game, right? Next to the other hookups you'll find a coaxial cable socket where you can plug into the TV system in the RV. If you plan to use cable hookups on your vacation, check with the rental company to find out whether a length of coaxial cable is included with your motorhome. Otherwise, be sure to bring a nice length of cable along with you.

That's it. You're all hooked up to electric, water, Wi-Fi, cable, and the beauty of your surroundings. The fact is that it's probably taken you longer to read this section than it will to get connected.

Now kick back, relax, explore the campground, chat with other campers, start a campfire, sip your favorite beverage. It's time to stop planning, stop worrying, and simply enjoy the beauty of the great outdoors!

## Breaking Camp

Of all the times that you are likely to damage your rented RV, breaking camp tops the list. There are so many little chores that need to be completed to make your motorhome roadworthy again, and failing to do even one of them can lead to paying a hefty repair bill to the owner, the campground, or both.

There's only one way to be sure that you are not the RVer that everyone tells stories about around the campfire: use a checklist. The checklist below is not comprehensive. Some items won't apply to your rental. Some may be missing. Be sure to add any items necessary that have been recommended by the RV's owner.

## Campground Departure Checklist

**INSIDE**

☐ Lower roof-mounted TV antenna

☐ Close roof vents and windows (except those left open for ventilation)

☐ Secure all loose items in the RV including:

- o   Bathroom counter
- o   Kitchen counters
- o   Bedroom headboard
- o   Tables
- o   Window sills

☐ Latch shower, closet doors, and all cabinet doors

☐ Latch refrigerator doors

☐ Stow and secure awnings

☐ Move items out of the slides' way inside the RV

☐ Move in slides and lock slide mechanism, if available

☐ Turn off all propane appliances except for refrigerator

☐ Discard all trash

☐ Check motorhome mirrors, and adjust if necessary

☐ If traveling with pets, make arrangements for their needs

**OUTSIDE**

☐ Collect and store all items from outside the RV (chairs, mats, toys, etc.)

☐ Empty black and gray tanks tank if necessary

☐ Close tank valves

☐ Add treatment chemicals and a small amount of water to black tank

☐ Disconnect and store cable TV wire

☐ Disconnect and store electrical cable

☐ Disconnect and store sewer hose and accessories

☐ Disconnect and store water hose in a sanitary compartment

☐ Raise or remove all stabilizing jacks if used

☐ Visually inspect under the RV for debris or personal items

☐ Check overall exterior of RV for protruding items

☐ Latch and lock all external RV compartments

☐ If carrying items (bicycles, etc.) on a hitch platform, load and secure them

☐ If towing and leaving permanently, hitch trailer or toad (towed vehicle) to motorhome

☐ If towing a small trailer or toad (towed car), ensure that it is hitched securely to motorhome, brakes are released, and all safety devices have been correctly applied

☐ Perform a final walk-around

☐ Leave marker in RV spot if returning (commonly a table, chairs, or a vehicle)

(You can download this list for free from www.completervrentalguide.com.)

# CHAPTER 10—THE RETURN

As all good things must come to an end, so must your RV vacation. Here are a few ideas to make the return process easier.

## The Night Before the Return

Since most RV rental agencies expect you to return your RV by mid-morning, it's a good idea to begin your preparations the night before. We've found that the most important part of this strategy is to stay in a campground located as close to the dealer as possible so that we have plenty of time in the morning to finish packing, assure that all tanks are emptied or refilled (depending on what you've agreed to in the rental agreement), have a nice breakfast, and make it to the return location with as little rush and stress as possible.

Pack everything that you won't need the next morning, and then store those packed suitcases in an outside storage compartment. Find any papers you'll need, such as your rental agreement, pre-rental inspection reports, and receipts for reimbursement, and put them where you can easily reach them when you get to the dealer.

Most importantly, whether you go out for dinner, have a campfire, or just sit and look at the stars, take some time to enjoy this last night of vacation and make it memorable.

**The Morning of the Return**

There's a lot to do your last morning, so be sure to allow plenty of time to get to the return location before their deadline, and plenty of time at the dealer for them to do a thorough inspection before they'll finish their paperwork and return your deposit. Remember, there will probably be others returning their RVs at the same time. Allow a minimum of an hour at the dealer before you need to leave for the airport if you're catching a plane. Budgeting extra time for every step along the way is the best way to reduce stress on the last morning of your vacation.

**Clean**—Too many campers have lost part or all of their deposit because of unexpected cleaning fees. Take time to get rid of all the trash and debris you've accumulated along the way. Most agencies expect you to return their RV "broom clean" but don't tell you exactly what that means. Unfortunately, some unscrupulous dealers will take advantage of that vague description to lay on extra charges at the end of the rental. You don't need to do a spit polish, but go ahead and wipe down all countertops and other surfaces that show dirt. Sweep all of the floors, and use a rag to wipe up any visible spills. If you are traveling with pets, use a special pet-hair brush to go over all of the upholstery and get rid of any pet hairs. Yes, I know the dealer is already charging you an extra "pet fee" for the extra cleaning that may be required. Still, do your best to make it look like Rover and Tabby have never been there.

**Inspect**—Do a quick inspection to check for any damage that may have occurred inside or outside the RV during your rental. If it's something simple that you can fix (such as a piece of molding that's pulled loose), go ahead and fix it. Walk through the RV, making sure that you open every door and drawer. Don't forget to look behind doors, too. It's easy to leave something in a drawer or pajamas hanging on a door hook!

**Unhook**—Today of all days it's important to use your campground departure checklist. Stress makes us forget things, and checklists make sure we remember. The two times you are most likely to drive off with a hatch open or cable hanging out are the first day and the last. Unless your rental agreement specifies that you can return the RV with waste in the black-water and gray-water tanks, make sure that you have properly emptied them. If for some reason you're not at a campground with a sewer hookup or dump station, you can go to www.rvdumps.com to find the nearest one you can use.

**Refill**—Your rental agreement probably requires that you return the RV with the fuel and propane tanks full. You may be able to refill the propane tank right at your campground. If not, ask the campground host to give you directions to the nearest business that sells propane, and make it your first stop upon leaving the campground. Top off with gas or diesel fuel while you're there or close to the rental return site. Many dealers charge triple the going rate per gallon if they have to fill the tank for you.

As soon as you arrive at the dealer, you can start to unload your personal belongings. This will make it much easier for them to complete their inspection promptly.

As the representative or owner does the inspection, be sure to have your copy of the pre-departure inspection report in hand, along with access to any pictures you took of items already damaged or missing. The inspection should be done in your presence. Don't accept an invitation from the owner to do the inspection later. If you know that you've damaged something, be upfront about it and point it out. You might think that they won't notice and you'll be off the hook for any repairs. Maybe. But they probably will notice, and it's going to make them much more likely to say "forget about it" if you've taken the high road and pointed out any damage before they find it themselves.

# CONCLUSION

That's it! I hope you have a great vacation!

If you have any comments, questions, corrections, or suggestions for this guide, please go to **www.completervrentalguide.com** and use the contact form, or email me at **jeff@completervrentalguide.com**. I'd also love to hear your stories and possibly include them in the next edition.

If you like this guide, please leave a review on **www.amazon.com** to help others who are still dreaming of their first RV vacation!

Happy travels, and God bless!

## Appendix A—RESOURCES AND LINKS

Free downloadable charts and checklists found in this book

**www.completervrentalguide.com**

## Boondocking

U.S Bureau of Land Management

**www.blm.gov**

Boondockers Welcome

**www.boondockerswelcome.com**

US Public Lands App

**http://www.twostepsbeyond.com/apps/uspubliclands/**

## Rentals

Cruise America

**www.cruiseamerica.com**

El Monte RV

**www.elmonterv.com**

Road Bear RV

**www.roadbearrv.com**

Bates International

**www.batesintl.com**

Camper Travel USA

**www.campertravelusa.com**

---

## Private Motorhome Rentals

**www.privatemotorhomerental.com**

Share My RV (California only)

**www.sharemyrv.com**

Craigslist

**www.craigslist.com**

---

## Itinerary Advice and Assistance

Trip Advisor

**www.tripadvisor.com**

Good Sam Club

**www.goodsamclub.com**

KOA Campgrounds

**www.koa.com**

Reserve America (National & Some State Parks)

**www.reserveamerica.com**

National Park Information

**www.nps.gov**

RV Park Reviews

**www.rvparkreviews.com**

Dump Station Locator

**www.rvdumps.com**

## Online Forums

Good Sam Club

**http://forums.goodsamclub.com**

Escapees

**www.rvnetwork.com**

iRV2

**www.irv2.com**

## Driving an RV

The New RV Driver Confidence Course

**https://www.youtube.com/watch?v=4CeThR_A4VI**

Made in the USA
Lexington, KY
04 August 2018